DISKO BAI

Nancy Campbell

DISKO BAY

ENITHARMON PRESS

First published in 2015
by Enitharmon Press
10 Bury Place
London WC1A 2JL

www.enitharmon.co.uk

Distributed in the UK by
Central Books
99 Wallis Road
London E9 5LN

Distributed in the USA and Canada
by Independent Publishers Group
814 North Franklin Street
Chicago, IL 60610
USA
www.ipgbooks.com

ISBN: 978-1-910392-18-8

Enitharmon Press gratefully acknowledges the financial support of
Arts Council England, through Grants for the Arts.

Individuals continue to sustain the Press through the
Enitharmon Friends Scheme. We are deeply grateful to all Friends,
particularly our Patrons: Colin Beer, Duncan Forbes, Sean O'Connor
and those who wish to remain anonymous.

British Library Cataloguing-in-Publication Data.
A catalogue record for this book is available
from the British Library.

Designed in Albertina by Libanus Press
and printed in England by
Short Run Press

CONTENTS

III. JUTLAND

I
DISKO BAY

The bird of prey flies with its wings backwards when it carries a feast
Traditional

UMIARISSAAT / THE SEAL PEOPLE

I watch four shadows pass the sun.
They are not men, those bearded ones
with fat, stooped heads and shining skin
aboard a boat with no beginning.

What brings such beasts? I do not know
their stooping forms; their short, fat arms that row
the endless boat; their long, white claws;
their round, black eyes that look to shore.

They row so close I see still more.
The round, black eyes that look to shore
have seen me watch. They are not men.
The boat will disappear again.

ASEQQUKU / FRAGMENT

A raven's wing at rest on the deep snow
remembers sunrise, the slow warm light
that grows behind the crags. Remembers flight
– plummet, beat and drift – and the low
confusion of wind in a distant nest.
No covert feathers could be blacker,
and frozen sinews do not fester
once the stained bone they cling to has lost
its body, sliced at the scapular.
Never to breed, never to scavenge
on scarlet seal hearts by the ice edge

KINGULERUTTUI / THE SURVIVORS

We settled here, scarcely believing our fortune
no more to skull the seas. The island was safe but
there were many deaths: driven by the darkness
men killed their kin; others drowned in shallow water

before they could reach the sea. The island was safe but
there was no earth to cultivate, nowhere to bury those men
killed by their kin. Bodies float in shallow water.
Corpses were left to rot, covered in rocks to hinder beasts:

there was no earth to hold them. Where could we hide the dead
when our sons were buried alive on the barren rock?
They were left to die, smothered in stones to keep them still;
the winter was their warder. Snow blew over the bones

of the firstborn buried alive on the highest rock.
The ice on those cairns was as good as a key in a lock:
the winter, their warder. Wind blew between the stones
and if sometimes it sounded like a child crying to be free

the ice on each cairn was as good as a key in a lock.
And so we settled, scarcely believing our fortune,
although it might sound as if we were crying to be free,
crying for a death to deliver us from darkness.

MALINGUARTOQ / THE DANCE

The hunter is a drunken fool;
    he bets, but rarely pays.
To win, he will break every rule
    in every game he plays.

The hunter wears a coat of skin
    and picks his blistered nose.
He won't remove his thrice-lined boots
    or change his underclothes.

He fumbles with a fraying cord
    to keep his temper calm.
The ends are knotted together,
    encircling his palm,
and his torn black nails weave in and out
    tangling the oily yarn.

Sometimes he sits so silently
    I forget that he is there
and I laugh and sing and sigh for him
    and unbraid my long black hair.

They say he was born too early,
    a caul upon his head.
I know his blood and mine run close,
    too close by far to wed,
yet I have lain all night with him
    in the narrow iron bed.

The animals watch for the hunter,
    but last night I saw him throw
the gloves of skin I sewed for him
    down to the dogs in the snow.

The old wounds open and start to weep
    on the hunter's hairless hands.
I ask why blood continues to seep
    though I staunch it with a band,
but he only mutters in his sleep
    those words I don't understand.

He travels miles across the ice
    yet never leaves his bed.
His cheeks are growing hollow;
    his eyes stare far ahead.

The animals wait. They are hungry
    but they trust he will follow the rest,
with an amulet in place of a gun
    clutched to his cold, clean chest.

SONG OF UKUAMAAT OF KAKILISAT
THE TERRIBLE MOTHER WHO LEFT FOX
PRINTS IN THE SNOW

Ernera, ernilijarsivara
tuugaaning assaqqoruteqanngitserng
Ernera ernilijarsivara
tuugaani nijaqorutaasaqanngitserng
nulijaaning assaarmigakku
taamalli ajunnguvarminaan.

My son, the man I made myself,
has no tattoos on his bony arms.
My son, the man I made myself,
will never wear an ivory crown.
I've stolen his only wife –
that's no mean feat for an old crone!

SONG OF ERLAVEERSINIOOQ
A FEMALE SHAMAN KNOWN AS 'THE ROBBER OF MEN'S INTESTINES'

Nailikkaataak sapangall, sapangallin
qivaaqinngivani sapangall
sapangallin

My cunt is hung,
hung with sea urchins.

My cunt bursts,
bursts with bladderwrack.

My cunt drips,
wet as a walrus snout.

My cunt is hungry.

SONG OF A WICKED WOMAN WHOSE KNOWLEDGE KNEW NO LIMIT

Uvijera kiillugu mikkissavan!
Kiillugu mikikkikki,
taana imaats qarsernun naqqulijukkumaarpan,
suuvalijukkumaarpan.

Kiillugu mikissavan, aaverling toqussuunga.
Tassa taamaaligima, toquguma
ummasunu pinaveerlinga mateernijarimaarparma.

Atamijaa ooqattaarimaarpan arn qisivanik.
Tass taamaatimik qarsilijern'jassuuti
taana naqqulijullugu, aataa taamaal
taasuminnga sakkeqalerivin toqukkumaarpan.

There's only one way to kill your enemy:

You must bite my clit off, pull it inside out,
and use it as an arrowhead.

Yes! Bite off my clit and pull it inside out,
but I warn you, I will bleed to death.

Hurry up! Blunt but hard,
it is the best blade for killing.

When I have bled to death,
cover me, for beasts will want to eat me.

Haft the head in soft driftwood
and fletch the shaft with folds of skin.

Yes, that's the arrow you need!
Only my weapon can kill your enemy.

ERSULLERAAPPOQ / HIDE AND SEEK

Towards the north of the island
   the hunter lives with his son
in a shed on stilts with a sunken roof.
   I live one house further on.

The sun sets behind the mountain.
   Dusk bleeds into the snow
and the shade cast by the hunter's house
   reaches my bare window.

From the harbour to the hillside
   only two transoms shine
and the wind slips like a knot between
   the hunter's house and mine.

My windows face the water
   frost grows across the glass.
I watch my own reflection drown
   in a deep lead of dark.

I cannot see around corners.
   I cannot see in the dark.
I cannot tell what moves beyond
these brittle panes of glass.

Is it a restless iceberg
   the tides have washed ashore,
this thing that intercepts the wind
   which suffocates my door?

The hunter draws a heavy blind
    as soon as day is done,
for his lamp would coat the moon with smoke
    and scorch the distant sun,

and in his single, sunken room
    he waits with his silent son,
but he tells no-one what he waits for
    though all know what he has done.

AJAKKAT / STICK AND PIN

Old leg, play the game.
The story changes every time
and is every time the same.

Tell your fortune hole by hole,
play the game of the hangman's tool
with an animal killed in June.

Tell it until there is nothing in the room
but a bone with ten holes drilled through it

and an antler hanging by a sinew from it
and a man who waits before he aims his throw:

he will hit the stab hole;
he will hit the whip hole;

the hole of healed wounds; the hole of crutches,
the lame, the fatally ill.

He who hits the stab hole must stab himself to death.
He who hits the whip hole may whip his wife to death.

And this is the hole where you may catch your breath.
And this the hole where you are put into the earth.

There is the hole of the crushed man
and the hole of the decomposing corpse.

The hole for the demolished home.
The hole of rust. The hole of steel.

The hole that allows you to remain in the game
and take another throw.

It is the game that no one desires to play.
It is the game we do not dare push away.

The company falls out, but he plays on.
Tonight he will capture the bride and bring her home.

AASAQ / SUMMER SONG

We'll feast on roseroot and bitter dandelion,
stems of fresh green angelica,
fine fresh angelica found in the shade,
dried capelin, dried cod and grey mattak:
a feast of fish and fruit to make us fat.

Those smoky silver fish will make us fat.

NAKUARSUUVOQ / THE NIGHT HUNTER

I am a poet. I am writing about Aua, the night hunter
and how his feet compact the snow and leave deep traces
as he passes my door destined for the harbour
where his boat is moored. I never see him. He might be a ghost

but that his feet compact the snow and leave deep traces.
When he is sleeping, as if by agreement I go to the shore
where his boat is moored. He might be a ghost. I never see him
emerge from the long darkness. In the brief daylight,

when he is sleeping, as if by agreement, I go to the shore.
I see drops of blood, and strange soft ochre things
emerge from the long darkness in the brief daylight.
The ice shelf bears the mark of sled and knife –

I see drops of blood, and strange soft ochre things.
All through the night none may yawn or wink an eye.
The ice shelf bears the mark of sled and knife.
The shaman tells the village, bound to him by hunger:

'All through the night none may yawn or wink an eye.'
I am a poet. I am writing about Aua, the night hunter
who is bound to the water, as I am bound to him by hunger.
I hear him pass my door, destined for the harbour.

THE HUNTER'S WIFE BECOMES THE SUN

'Don't go without this.' Isabel handed me a small white box
which held a candlestick and four attendant angels.
Jingling clichés punched from sheets of tin,
the angels turn, propelled by heat rising from a candle,
and hooked by their haloes from wires as if the darkness
were a deep pool for fly-fishing, and my window

delicate as ice upon its surface. Spinning by the window,
this carousel recalls a childhood blessing: *Four angels
at my head.* If they came to life, like the small white angels
who fought the Snow Queen's snowflakes, would their tin
armour frighten bears back to the polar darkness?
Whose are the gifts they grasp: tree, star, trumpet, candle?

Only the undertaker sells the right kind of candle
to suit these angels. At home, he wreathes a small white coffin
with plastic lilies, but says nothing. His window
overlooks crucifixes buried in snow; there are no angels
on the graves of the Danes, who came to barter tin
for ivory and sealskin. Their eyes brimmed with darkness,

you see it in old photographs. Sleepless in the darkness,
I read their letters home, those 'tragic accidents'. Green candles
burn beyond the hills: the dead are dancing. The window
between the worlds grows thin. A solar wind blows its low tin whistle
and fire draws closer. Soon Earth will be a small white dwarf,
a revolving toy abandoned by its guardian angels.

The candle gutters. Lynched in their own light, the angels
hang still. Each holds her gift before her as if the tin
scorched her fingertips. Heat has melted the small white stump
to nothing. Once, they say, this land was lit by candles

made of ice, when water burned, glazing the darkness
of endless night. Day had not dawned on any window.

The hunter spoke. His cold breath quenched a candle:
'In darkness we are without death.' His wife listened
and replied, 'But we need more light, not darkness,
while we are alive.' She seized a shard of incandescent ice
and rose into the sky, scattering a vast white wake
of stars, which some might say were angels,

if, in temperate darkness, we still believed in angels.
The small seal and the white whale know we're just tin gods.
At the world's last window, I light another candle.

ALAGASSAQ / THE LESSON

I place my fingers round his neck and feel
his gorge rise – or is he swallowing
his tongue? He wants to teach me the word
for 'welcome'. Suddenly, he's trembling:
his larynx rumbles, then his breath is gone.
He asks me to remember those vibrations,
and, anxious as a nurse who takes a pulse,
touches my throat to judge its contortions.
Will I ever learn these soft uvulars?
I'm so eager, I forget that the stress
always falls on the second syllable.
My echo of his welcome is grotesque.
He laughs, an exorcism of *guillemets*,
dark flocks of sound I'll never net, or say.

ukiigatta last winter.

ukioq the winter; the whole year.

   ukiukkut in winter; during the year.

   ukiuuppaa the winter came upon her before she reached home, or finished building her house.

ukiorippoq she has a good winter; it is a good winter.

ukiorpoq the winter has come.

ukiortaaq the new year.

OQQERSUUT / THE MESSAGE

Since I can't post a letter this far north,
I'm sending you an Arctic snowstorm,
the worst weather London's ever known:
deep drifts resisting shovel, salt and thaw.

Since I can't touch your winter skin
I appoint the most delicate snowflakes
to fall into your arms, kiss your cold face
and silence the city I loved you in.

I can't judge your heart's temperature,
although I lay out the last glacier
over the miles between us. Don't you hear
the wind? It calls to know your nature.

It's warmer than you think, for I have dressed
that wild inquisitor in my own breath.

> *Can you bind the chains of the Pleiades?*
> *Can you loosen Orion's belt?*
>   Job 38:31

Hard to begin but a beginning must be made:
the bed risen from, boots pulled on,
the door opened to the wind
and snow blown in by night brushed away.

November.
                    There will be storms at sea.
The body, cumbersome after a god's grace,
barely musters breath.

Always judgement on the return,
double tracks by the shore.

Use your blade to wound the bone
not to whittle wood.

One less.
One more.

        *

Before the quotas, boasting.
The hunters came home singing.

Now whispers trail off,
silent letters on a cloth ear.

Numbers are nothing here.
Sad and secret now, no more catch-share.

*

Men come with clipboards once a year.
They collect and they confer.

We do not see the kill,
we do not see the keeping.

Let us accumulate evidence
without passion or prejudice.

The ice edge is his factory:
Ravens peck the wretched mess

wires to cause distress,
props of death.

Pitted snow
blood, phlegm, tar, spit, stone.

Wire rack, strung on palings: rusted.
Lichen, where ice reveals the rock: rusted.

Note this. Rust is the age of metal
and rust runs in all metal.

*

Orion walks on water
while wise men wait in the harbour.

Limbs pinned with light
he is burning up, his belt burning him
as he strides towards dawn.

Cities obscure him. Greater than their grids
he turns
                     the world is gone.

Does he long for the smell of the earth,
the blood of the hare and the lion on his hands?
Does he remember where the owls breed?

The hunters are his.
The hunters' hearts are his.
Hearts of sinew, hearts of ice.

KITSISSUT / THE COLONY

'Evolution values survival of the fittest over kindness
so people are cruel here,' the Danish doctor tells me,
'It is a harsh place to bring up children.
To summon spring, the islanders sing from the mountain.'

People are cruel here: the Danish doctor tells me
those who miss the ceremony must die within the year.
To summon spring, the islanders sing from the mountain,
'Great sun, please settle smiling on our land.'

Those who miss the ceremony will die within the year
yet old men drink in darkness instead of singing
'Great sun, please settle smiling on our land.'
The song is tuneless. The children do not know the words

yet old men drink in darkness instead of singing.
I am exhausted by the ascent. We begin squabbling, since
the song is tuneless, the children do not know the words.
Our feet sink in the snow; the sun will melt our tracks.

I cannot complete the ascent. We begin squabbling, since
evolution values survival of the fittest over kindness.
I stumble in the snow. There will be no traces.
This is a harsh place to bring up children.

i

Where does the Arctic end? Asked how far south
the region reaches, scholars disagree.
Today the Circle sweeps around the globe
at a latitude of sixty-six degrees,
and, though the north was first named αρκτικός
or 'Land of the Great Bear' by ancient Greeks
after the seven stars that turn above,
it now excludes James Bay, where true bears breed.
Experts argue that the northern treeline,
first patch of permafrost, or – in July –
the fifty degree isotherm define
where temperate becomes arctic, but why
specify an ambit when the axis,
the Geographic Pole, is in constant flux?

ii

The Geographic Pole is never still:
the slow lure of lunar gravity,
tectonic shifts, river sediment stirred
by spate – all tilt the globe slightly
on its axis, so that the Pole migrates
sixty-five feet around an unmarked space
known as the Chandler Circle; it navigates
its rivals – the Geomagnetic
and Magnetic Poles, and the Northern Pole
of Inaccessibility (a name
now obsolete). Cartographers locate
this roving Pole beyond coordinates.
Here, where all lines of longitude begin
drift ice obscures the Arctic's origin.

II
RUIN ISLAND

*Our tales are narratives of human experience, and therefore
they do not always tell of beautiful things*
Osarqaq

A SERPENT, A SKELETON AND A STONE

Sail out to sea while the day is young
scale the cliffs with your hands alone
search the caves as the sun goes down
and bring back home
a serpent, a skeleton and a stone.

With the serpent, strike your wife
with the skeleton, feed her
then carve her a lamp out of the stone.

When she has felt the serpent's bite,
swallowed a skin with the bones all in
seen a lamp that has not known the sun
your wife will bear a child

but he will be mine
and I will name him after a dead one.

READING THE WATER

Make the boy a kayak
from a speckled skin

let him hold a paddle
strap him safely in

take him to the shore
point the prow to sea

launch him in the shallows
and count to three.

Out of the darkness
seals will rise

to gauge their deaths
within his eyes.

They'll stare as if
he is one of their own

and dive back down
when you pull him home.

QUJAAVAARSSUK HEARS ADVICE FROM A MAN
WHO IS NOT HIS FATHER

Listen to me, Qujaavaarssuk
        sometimes others will contend with you
        and sometimes they'll tell lies

sometimes a stronger man will claim he was first to hear the whale breathing
        even when he knows you heard it by night
        and he did not hear it until dawn

sometimes the men in your own boat will mock you
        and you'll hear loud laughter
        when all you wish to hear is your wife's singing

and sometimes your limbs will feel heavy, the sea will launch itself on your boat
        filling it with water before you can leave the shore
        and while you are bailing, others will reach the hunting grounds.

Qujaavaarssuk, these things are hard, but they do not bring hunger.
        Hunger will come of its own accord.

THE STRONG MAN SINGS A DIRGE AT THE FISHING GROUNDS

Below the dark cliffs, the wide water
below the wide water, the black seal
within the black seal, the red fish
within the red fish, the white wing
within the white wing, the first ice
under the first ice, the old sun
under the old sun, the dark cliffs.

THE STRONG MAN SHOWS QUJAAVAARSSUK
HOW TO DIVIDE THE CATCH

I'll take the head
the tusk and the guts
the breast and the back
a flipper, a shoulder
and the side my harpoon struck.

You take the other side
the lungs, the heart
and half the tail.

Him over there
give him the other half-tail.

There's nothing for the others.

HOSPITALITY

It was a hard winter
and there was hunger in the south.

The hunters who had nothing
heard of Qujaavaarssuk
the strong man's son who never went hungry
the strong man's son who caught two seals
every time he went hunting.

The hungry ones came to his table
and he fed them the kidneys of a black seal
as the sea ice hardened.

THE DAY THE TIDES FROZE

Qujaavaarssuk shuddered.
It was as cold inside as it was outside.
It was colder on land than it was on the sea.
His spit froze before it hit the ground.

The sea turned pale. It heaved and hardened
until there was not a fissure wide enough for a seal
to poke its nose through.

Qujaavaarssuk watched their shadows
moving beneath the ice.
                    Then they were gone
and he set out to the ice edge to follow them.

IN DANGER OF SNOW BLINDNESS

Qujaavaarssuk looked ahead to the horizon
and saw ice.

No dark sky reflecting the open sea,
no blood but the sun's.

He looked back to land
and saw ice.

                One word
was enough to turn the dogs.

That was the first night he came home
his sled empty, his kamiks clean.

It was time to let the lamps burn out
and take up the drum.

THE LAST SEAL

There was nothing left to feed the dogs.
Qujaavaarssuk shot them, one by one
and fed them to each other.

Birds no longer flew overhead
and people gnawed on old bones.

The settlement grew silent.
Only Qujaavaarssuk still had meat
in his winter cache.

He cut a black seal in two
and hauled one half to Tugto's house.
The house had become a foxhole,
there were no tracks leading to it
no tracks leading away from it.

Qujaavaarssuk flung in the tail first and then the blubber
so Tugto could see it.
He crept in after, and called to Tugto's wife
'I ask you to remove this ice.'

THE STRONG MAN SPREADS A RUMOUR

Wise women are never uncertain.
They have no need to lie to us
as their faith is stronger than ours.
They sweep the house and do their chores
and always, underneath, they scheme.

They terrify us when they are in a vengeful mood.
They try to punish us.
Their beliefs lead them to do damage
and create accidents.

They can be helpful
but they kill, like all the wise ones.
This is why people fear them.
They kill secretly:
no one knows when it will happen

nor how it will happen.
When they sense evil in the air
they send their demons.
There are no visible acts of violence.
They work their menace with what they hold within them.

SPEAKING TO THE SUN

She knows she will be taken from her sewing
or from stewing angelica
and although she is thin as an ice pick
and as impossible to wound
we will find her heart.

We must bury her before
our fingers begin to turn black,
before her screams are forgotten
and the birds settle on the cliff again.
We must sever her head
and hide it in a fissure
where ice parts from ice.

When spring comes
her head will show the sun how strong we are,
her head will tell the story of her death.

Epilogue

WORDS SPOKEN BY A HUNTER
WHO CAN NO LONGER HEAR THE QUESTION

Ungasitsimu adjaa
angadjavingisarparpun.

Sinittarijartarpungu ukijimiliiniin,
qiijanartorsuvasimmi, ujaqqat ataa...
aterujuvanun.

Ilikkardjungu aama
tujorminart'qanngilaq.

When we were young
no place seemed too far away for hunting.

We travelled a long way,
too far to come back the same day.
We slept in stone caves
and were cold in winter.

Nothing is too harsh
when you are accustomed to it.

III
JUTLAND

Siunissaq nalunartorsuuvoq – the future is full of riddles

JUTLAND

Some objects, not hooked out
with a hazel branch or stolen by chancers,
were discovered when a farmer
decided to rake the rich earth down
towards his pasture, levelling the mound
shovelful by shovelful, until he reached stone
and then something that was not stone.
    'There are no natural hills here,'
the priest told him, when he came
to beg paper. He sat an hour after dinner
scratching a letter to the museum director.
That night he dreamed of tree trunks
that split and then closed again,
shutting him in like a coffin.
The director dispatched a memo
to the department of antiquities:
'Colleagues! Who *wants* to go?'
(What luck that Petersen was sent.)
By cab, by steamer, staying overnight in inns . . .
at last he rolled up in a hired cart
along the high road, passing fields
in which all work had stopped
when the rumours began.

He climbed at once into the pit
and saw the water leaching from the bole.
He took neat notes, to say where things
were found, and what was found and what
was not. He ordered photographic plate.
A little late but dutiful all the same
he telegraphed the director
who notified the king.
                          A local boy

was set to watch the mound both night and day:
there was no longer very much to take away
but Petersen was sure he would find more
than just blue dust. (What part of us
can last three thousand years?)
He gave the order to keep digging,
to open the tree trunks.

The director was unprepared
for Petersen's second telegram
celebrating rare evidence of human life,
not stolen, not yet decomposed:
'Peculiar coffin. Animal hide. Cap, cloaks,
shirt, foot covering, sword, sheath, 2 fibulae:
all well preserved.
                    Am digging for wife.'

PROVERBS OF WATER

It's quiet here. Is it too quiet for you? The rain is soft as the conversations of coral.

*

We used to swim by the dam, and pull little fish out of our swimsuits. Then my friend started to get ill.

*

The thief of birdsong tries to capture the colour of rain. It's just grey, he complains.

*

A book bound in bricks, a scallop shell concertina. One is too heavy for this place, the other too light.

*

An empty bucket is always a bad omen. Turn back, if you see one at the outset of your journey.

*

It is kindest to measure depth in metres. A fathom is the span of a man's outstretched arms. The fjord, two fathoms deep, drowns his embrace.

*

Wave dragon, wave star, now the pier leads nowhere.

*

Wind blows waves across the road. We drive on a silver river. It takes one hour to reach the sun.

*

My lover is wary of water. *The car started to sink so quickly.*

The water is a loyal silence on all our heels. I'm lost. Give me the grey key again, the sea that tolls the truth.

*

It is easier to look at the stones than the sea, until salt spatters your spectacles.

*

We drank from blue china. The saucer did not match the teacup: two sets must have got mixed up years ago. We sipped, and consulted marine charts.

*

The coast is new as a foetus and old as a fossil. The bedrock rebounds from the glacier's weight. Sea bewilders it.

*

A colony of herons, of rare and timid animals can be mentioned, the birch mouse and otter.

*

Dunes are the most fickle of landforms, ever blowing inland from the sea, ever on the move.

*

Two blind oxen, bound together, once rested here. The church is dark but through one window water dances.

*

Find a fish to catch a fish. There's nothing worse than a bare hook. Mussels are thirsty for the sea.

Where have the eels gone? There's a hint of net in the water, a line of floats and a black flag.

*

A stone pulled up on a hook should be kept on land. A knot in a tangled line may not be undone.

*

To cure seasickness: Eat seaweed. Smell rose root. Tickle your throat with a feather dipped in cod liver oil. Cut grass in a churchyard and place it in your shoes before sailing.

*

You will know when you come to the river.

*

After the funeral wood anemones were thrown upon the lake.

*

Who climbs highest, the skylark or the snail?

*

If you keep fossils in your study, will you grow wiser, or just older?

*

When you're tired, water makes a sound like sleep
and nothing happens and nothing happens and water
sounds   like silence

CONVERSATIONS

A combination of things

I think it's a combination of things
it's climate change yes
and it's forestry taking out too many trees
and lorries tearing down the slope with the logs on them
and the streams running straight down the hillside now
and the farmers not allowed to look after the riverbanks like they
                                                    used to
not dredging, not taking the gravel out onto the bank
and all the weeds in the river
and they're building on flood plains which they were never
                                        allowed to do before

I don't think it is one thing
I think it is a combination of things
a combination of everything

Hindsight

Soon as it starts to rain
you're looking for water.
We've got the barriers now.
They do help
but they could probably do
with being a tiny bit higher.
We were flooded last year
but not to danger level.
We had to move out in any case.
Just for the day.

Planning permission

It's happening all over.
If it happens again, I'll live upstairs –
and downstairs, I'll cement it out.
I could even have a garden downstairs.

Selling the house is hard.
You can't just say 'I'm moving'
and go somewhere else
when no one wants to move in.

So I think about other things:
driving a boat instead of a car,
keeping bookshelves on pulleys,
growing flowers in a cement garden.

LEGENDS

Bexhill, I think it was, a brooding town,
bitter as a fag-end between the lips,
where roads of shut-up houses by the shore
ended at a theatre we'd been hired to fill.

It was a winter afternoon without
a morning, and the ukuleles gone
for fish & chips and shelter from the wind
in groups of three and two and utterly out of tune.

Already dressed for several minor parts
we turned from the pavilion and raced
towards the waves' applause. Black lace,
fishnets and watered silk lagged on the tide

as we rolled far out for a long time,
pretending to be seals. 'Encore!' a gull called
and the grey surge dragged us north,
crying in vain to distant fishermen.

When we staggered from the sea again,
the chill sand splintered our feet
and our clothes clung to us like selkie skin.
A boat was pulled up on the shingle,

tilting from the shore to the stony scree,
slowly amassing salt spray and driftwood,
blue string and bladderwrack in its dark hull.
I read my name on its keel.

TWO OLD RIDDLES

i

Wiht cwom æfter wege   wrætlico liþan
cymlic fr ceole   cleopode to londe
hlinsade hlude –   leahtor wæs gryrelic
egesful on earde   ecge wæron scearpe
wæs hio hetegrim   hilde to sæne
biter beadoweorca   bordweallas grof
heardhiþende   heterune bond
sægde searocræftig   ymb hyre sylfre gesceaft
is min modor   mæg da cynnes
þæs deorestan   is dohtor min
eacen uploden   swa þæt is ældum cuþ
firum on folce   seo on foldan sceal
on ealra londa gehwam   lissum stondan

She advanced from the sea, sir.
Wrested from the waves, it seemed –
a stunner, for sure.
Sent a shiver down my spine to see her.
As she approached the shore she mocked us
with a fusillade that ricocheted against
the trembling earth. It was a grim salvo.
I watched as sharp blades, honed with malice
but battle-slack, scored our wooden defences.
Her orders to strike were encrypted.
She spoke slyly of her origins, in words I could not understand:
'My mother – the dearest of our race –
is my daughter, who grows ever greater.
Wise men the world over know
she will remain after them on Earth,
spreading silently over the forgetful land.'

ii

Hwilum ic gewite,   swa ne wenaþ men,
under yþa geþræc;   eorþan secan,
garsecges grund.   Fifen biþ gewreged,
fam gewealcen   *   *   *
hwælmere hlimmeð,   hlude grimmeð,
streamas staþu beatað,   stundum weorpaþ
on stealc hleoþa   stane ond sonde,
ware ond wæge,   þonne ic winnende,
holmmægne biþeaht,   hrusan styrge,
side sægrundas.   Sundhelme ne mæg
losian ær mec læte   se þe min latteow bið
on siþa gehwam.   Saga, þoncol mon,
þonne streamas   eft stille weorþað,
yþa geþwære,   þe mec ær wrugon.

Sometimes I dive deep beneath the waves,
farther than men can fathom, discovering
abyssal plains. The sleeping swells stir,
rollers start to foam...
The whispering whale's wake rises with a roar
and breakers beat at the edges of the earth
slinging stones and sand, rocks and strands of kelp
against the steep cliffs, while I endure
the weight of water above me,
black smokers shuddering on the sea bed.
I shall never be free of this salt shroud
until a true pilot commands my course.
Wise man, name the one
who will draw me from the ocean's hold
when the tides have turned on their traces
and the currents are calm once more.

TWO NEW RIDDLES

i

I cut the ocean from a cherry tree.
It was invisible to everyone but me
until I washed each wave in water.
With every wash the waves grew darker
and dirtier, and the tides traced lines
over a floating mass of land
where bushes bend to meet the waves:
their cracked bark, beaten smooth,
casts no watery reflection
but only acts as mirror to my ocean.

ii

Only gods can be resurrected.
Everything else is fossilised.
Sooner or later we all turn to stone.
I'll never tell you lies.

Show me a mirror in which
you see no reflection;
a blackness in which
many colours hide.

Show me a knot of bone
a heaviness easy to hold
a spiral without centre
and I will show you lies.

It is valuable to none:
neither man-made nor useful.
No longer alive.
It's a lure, it's a clue,

it's both truth and speculation.
An aperture on age
that will not open.
It is its own burial stone.

WILLIAM SCORESBY JUNIOR DREAMS OF HIS WIFE MARY ELIZA WHILE SAILING OFF THE EAST COAST OF GREENLAND IN 1822

my darklight, I bottlenose you

       my flat-aback, I fid you

my fox, I careen you

       my galliot, I junk you

my lipper, I mallemuch you

       my piggin, I chop you

my preventer, I clinch you

       my ancient, I double you

my guess-warp, I am coming-home

GIVING UP ON CAPITALISM

The first kayak he made was a one-krone kayak,
one krone was all he got for it.
He threw the coin down on his mother's bench:
fifty øre for coffee and sugar,
fifty øre for needles.

The next kayak he made was a two-kroner kayak,
he was given two kroner for it.
He ran to lay the coins on his mother's palm:
one krone for whisky,
one krone for blue cotton.

Then he made a kayak all for himself.
He had only enough skins
to cover a slim hull
but he pegged them down deftly
and paddled away.

NOTES

Page 9: *Umiarissaat* are the vindictive spirits of dead seals. They come from the sea on boats of ice to exact revenge on hunters' wives.

Page 14: During the 1950s the oral historian Maliaraq Vebæk collected stories from elderly speakers of the Qavak dialect in the settlements of Cape Farewell, South Greenland. These settlements have subsequently been abandoned and the Qavak dialect has become extinct. Song is a central element of Greenlandic culture, and many of the storytellers enhanced their narratives with lyric interludes. The original Qavak versions of these three songs, which record the voices of legendary female characters, were performed by Juliane Mouritzen, Martin Mouritzen and Therkel Petersen.

Page 35: Quoted by Knud Rasmussen in *Greenland by the Polar Sea* (New York: Frederick A. Stokes Co., n.d.).

Page 46: The epilogue is taken from an interview with Jorsias Ammosen from *Southernmost People of Greenland, Dialects and Memories* by Maliaraq Vebæk, Man & Society Vol. 33 (Copenhagen: The Commission for Scientific Research in Greenland, 2006).

Page 47: *Greenlandic–English Dictionary* (Copenhagen: Meddelelser om Grønland Bind LXIX, C.a. Reitzels Forlag, 1927).

Page 57: This riddle and the one following can be found in *The Exeter Book*, as riddles number 6 (iceberg) and 2 (tsunami).

Page 59: Answer: *Japanese woodblock artist working on a print.*

Page 60: Answer: *ammonite.*

ACKNOWLEDGEMENTS

These poems were begun during a residency at Upernavik Museum, Greenland, and completed during a Hawthornden Fellowship. Both periods of writing were made possible with funding from Arts Council England.

The three Qavak songs were first published in *qaartsiluni*; they were nominated for the 2012 Pushcart Prize. 'The night hunter' was awarded second prize in the Norman MacCaig Centenary Poetry Competition, and subsequently published as an artist's book designed by Roni Gross and Peter Schell of Z'roah Press in 2011. Roni Gross chose 'The lesson' as the text for her work commemorating the bombing of Al-Mutannabi Street, Baghdad, published as *Tikilluarit* by Z'roah Press in 2013. 'The hunter's wife becomes the sun' was first published in the Candlestick Press anthology *The Twelve Poems of Christmas (Volume Six)* edited by Carol Ann Duffy. 'Conversations' was commissioned by Hexham Book Festival.

I am grateful to the editors of *Dark Mountain Journal*; *Ink, Sweat and Tears*; *The Interpreter's House*; *Magma*; *Modern Poetry in Translation*; *Moving Worlds*; *Mslexia*; *Oxford Poetry* and *The Rialto* in which the other poems first appeared, and to Stephen Stuart-Smith at Enitharmon Press who guided the manuscript to publication.

My thanks to Alexander Cigale, Katy Evans-Bush, MacGillivray, Helena Nelson, Bethan Stevens, Ruth Valentine and Anna Zvegintzov for their close reading; to the staff of The Lit & Phil Library, Newcastle and the Scott Polar Research Institute, Cambridge (in particular Heather Lane); and to the unknown bookseller at Daunt Books in Holland Park who sold me a copy of *Arctic Dreams* by Barry Lopez.

This book could not have been completed without the kindness of the following people: in Denmark Mette-Sofie D. Ambeck, Liz and Lars Hempel-Jørgensen; in Greenland Beathe Møldrup, Ole Gamst-Pedersen, Karen and Ole Thorleifsen; in Iceland Helena Dejak, Kristján Jóhannsson, Örlygur Kristfinnsson, Guðný Róbertsdóttir, Björn Valdimarsson and Lefteris Yakoumakis; in the UK Sarah Bodman, Helen Barr, Isabel Brittain, Colin and Anne Campbell, Kenneth and Eithne Campbell, Hannah Cole, Dennis Harrison, Pippa Hennessy, Ralph Kiggell, Frances and Nicolas McDowall, Paul Preece, Carinne Piekema and Mark Walton. To all of them, and above all to Anna Zvegintzov, who never expected to learn Greenlandic: *qujanaq*.